Campfire
Publishing

Jekyll Says More!

Lessons & Trends for Felines & Friends

D.C. Blackbird

Jekyll Says More!
Lessons & Trends for Felines & Friends!

by
D.C. Blackbird

This book was written for my feline companion named Jekyll. The characters, incidents, and dialogues were inspired by Jekyll and other companion cats in our home, or are the products of the author's imagination. Any resemblance to actual events, or locales, or persons, or felines, in Kittyland or Humanland, or cats outside of our home, is entirely coincidental.

Profits from the sale of this book benefit animal adoption, care, liberation, rescue, and welfare organizations. If you know of any such organizations that would like to sell this book as part of its fundraising efforts, please contact the Publisher at **WelcomeToKittyland.com**.

Jekyll Illustrations by Christine P. Flores

Graphic Design by Leah Frieday

Dedication

"Jekyll Says More!" is dedicated to all the non-human animals who have ever been eaten, harmed, hunted, murdered, and/or tortured anywhere, anytime, around the world, throughout history.

This book is specifically dedicated to Jekyll, Radar, Autumn, Smudge, Gizmo, Jasper, Annabelle, Double-Stuff, Buddy, and of course their Human Mom who loved Jekyll more than the words in this book, or any other, can fully express.

Table of Contents

Foreword

If you are reading this, then you likely enjoyed my first book, **"Jekyll Says ... Good Deeds Cats Do, That You Should, Too!"** If not, then kindly allow me to tell you about myself. My name is Jekyll. I was born in North Carolina in 1999. I was found as a baby in a dirty ditch because no one wanted me. Even though I was really small, and adorable, and at the time I even had bright blue eyes as baby kitties like me tend to have. It is difficult to believe that I was abandoned on the side of the road as if I was worthless garbage. How could anyone treat another living being like that? Especially when one notices the unique marking on my face. Everyone knows that a special marking means great things await those who have them. A marking like mine meant that I was destined to be blessed with good fortune and would develop miraculous skills, talents, and gifts. Without a doubt, I was favored to have a treasure trove of happy and wondrous days. After all, many of the great heroes of mythology and folklore had birthmarks or special markings. Clearly, good fortune awaited me!

As was preordained, two wonderful Humans took me into their home. I was brushed off, freshened up, my trusty tuxedo was cleaned, and I was given boodles of food, water, and love. They raised me in a fun and affectionate household. When I first arrived, I had the best big brother (Radar) and sister (Autumn) that anyone could want! And soon I had many more! What a wonderful family! We were always singing and dancing and playing! With their endless affection, encouragement, and support, I was able to follow my dreams and become all I was destined be. Boy, oh, boy! Whoever threw me away really missed out! And you are missing out, too, unless you go to a shelter and adopt a homeless cat or dog. Even if you already have one or two (like my Humans did), perhaps you can find it in your heart to take in another, and give him or her a loving home. They need you.

I supervised the writing and publication of this book so I could share with you some of the tips that helped me become the envy of kitties everywhere on earth and in Kittyland. Please read the following poems slow, and aloud, so they sound best. Whether you are a Kitty, Doggie, Furry Critter, or a Human—if you follow my simple tips, you can be happy, healthier, and successful, too!

Paws, Purrs, Licks, & Kisses!

Jekyll 🐾🐾

Jekyll Says More!

Welcome back, friend. It's great you're here.
"Jekyll Says More!" And now you'll hear.
Make yourself at home. Step right in.
It's so great to see you again.

Please, please me with your pleas for more.
Helping you is what I'm here for.
Remember to read poems aloud.
And you'll float like a fluffy cloud.

Poetry is so great to read.
Treat each word as if it's a seed.
Respect and care for them real well.
And you'll be cast under their spell!

You read my first book. I'm so glad.
And now you've got this one to add.
This second book will teach you more.
To win in life and get top score!

Are you ready? Get set and go!
Here's some wisdom you'll want to know.
So sit back and hear each word here.
And all lessons will be quite clear.

LESSONS & TRENDS
FOR FELINES
& FRIENDS!

Find Time to Play!

Jekyll says to "Find time to play."
Each and every wonderful day.
Don't let your work cloud up your mind.
Sometimes you need to just unwind.

Stop and smell roses as a plan.
Swim in the water. Kick the can.
Play with friends or when you're alone.
Enjoy silence. Get off the phone!

Go spend a whole day without words.
Riding a bike or watching birds.
Go play somewhere that is hush-hush.
Spend time wisely and do not rush.

Love the Little Things!

Jekyll says, "Love the little things."
With furry fur and feathered wings.
Blades of grass with cool drops of dew.
And neighbors that say, "Howdy-do!"
Kitties, Doggies, and tiny Bugs.
All of them deserve lots of hugs!
Little plants need attention, too.
And baby cows that give a moo.

Little moments make life ideal.
Walks on the shore fill one with zeal.
What is your favorite "little thing?"
Do you know what makes your heart sing?
Quiet moments sure are the best.
Like watching birds building a nest.
Love the little things all the time.
It will open your heart and mind.

Love Nature's Beauty!

Jekyll says, "Love nature's beauty."
Swim in lakes and eat things fruity.
Roll in the grass when it is warm.
Stay under roofs when there's a storm.

Mosey along through woods nearby.
Watch from afar as bluebirds fly.
Go hiking through green mountain trails.
Check out a leaf and its details.

Snakes! Skunks! Snails! Sparrows in blue skies.
Nature is a feast for your eyes!
Never do damage. Never kill.
Don't harm a bird or an ant's hill.

The Earth was here
way before you.
So leave her nothing
to undo.

Care for Those You Love

Jekyll says, "Care for those you love."
Family, friends, and those you think of.
Friends can be the luck of the draw.
So choose them wisely—paw-to-paw.

Do fun things they all want to do.
The usual, or something new.
Favorite people bring happiness.
Family and friends sure are priceless!

Be Kind to All Things
Big & Small!

"Be kind to all things big and small."
Jekyll says that to one and all!
When you see critters that need aid.
Go and help them. Don't be afraid!

Always be a goody two-shoes.
You can be kind if you so choose.
If you see critters in distress.
Be their hero and nothing less.

Help a bird that falls from a tree.
Help it heal till it can fly free.
Every thing you see wants to live.
Love and help is what you can give.

Adopt a cat. Adopt a dog.
Don't eat a cow. Don't eat a frog.
If roles reversed, you'd want the same.
Saving a life means more than fame.

Slow Down

Jekyll says, "Slow down. Chew with care."
You know the tortoise beat the hare!
Please take your sweet time when you eat.
Don't have a meal while on your feet.

Don't watch TV when gobbling food.
You may pig out and be quite rude!
Chew once. Chew twice. Chew really well.
Savor flavors. Enjoy the smell.

Take the time to enjoy hot tea.
Your life will change. Just watch and see.
You get one body in your life.
Don't cause it pain. Don't cause it strife.

No need for you to gulp or slurp.
It's not polite for you to burp.
Take your time and enjoy your meal.
You'll be surprised how good you feel.

Enjoy Fresh Air

Jekyll says to "Enjoy fresh air."
Feel the cool breeze blow through your hair!
Open your windows every night.
Watch shooting stars under moonlight.

Take a stroll in the afternoon.
Gather flowers for a festoon.
Breathing in slow will hit the spot.
Take in a little or a lot.

Nothing is better than fresh air.
For you to enjoy everywhere.
So close your eyes and breathe in slow.
In rain, or shine, or sleet, or snow.

Live a Simple Life

Jekyll says, "Live a simple life."
Sit on the grass and play a fife.
You don't need rings or fancy cars.
Just time at night to look at stars.

No need for mansions or huge bills.
A quaint house can give the same thrills.
Don't rush to buy the latest thing.
The best gift is a song to sing.

You sure do not need bric-a-brac.
Don't let your home look like a shack.
You do not need every gewgaw.
Turn from "things" with your tooth and claw!

Don't get hung up on buying stuff.
You'll never feel you'll have enough.
The best things in life sure are free.
Don't think so now? Some day you'll see.

How 'bout a bike ride with a friend?
Bring bread and fruit around the bend.
Happiness simply can't be bought.
Live simply and find all you've sought.

Tend to a Garden

Jekyll says that gardens change lives.
Respect butterflies and beehives.
Your spring flowers will grow brightly.
If you take care, they'll grow nightly.

Your veggies will soon grow strongly.
Just please don't water them wrongly.
If you want great soil all around.
Then put squirmy worms in the ground.

Don't use pesticides. None at all.
Some bugs will fly in. Some will crawl.
You can have green thumbs or green paws.
Just follow nature's earthly laws.

A garden gives freedom to eat—
Healthy bright food, and not dead meat.
Start right now. Don't wait anymore.
Grow the things you see in the store.

If you have no land — pots will do.
Make no excuses to stop you.
If Jekyll says it, then it's right.
His advice will make your life bright!

Read Each Night & Day

Jekyll says, "Read each night and day."
And learn what others have to say.
Fill your shelves with great manuscripts.
They'll take you on amazing trips.
Grasp history and science, too.
And you'll learn things you never knew.
Good books will glue you to your seat.
Read of Troy and the Grecian fleet!
Reading is a wise thing to do.
It's time well spent—you know it's true.
Grab some books. Turn off that TV.
Words are worth gold and they are free!

Afterword

The central motivation to write this book was to immortalize Jekyll. We did not want him to be forgotten. He deserves more than that. He was special and there are lessons that cats and humans can learn from the fine examples he set in his extraordinary life.

Jekyll left Humanland on June 6, 2011 in order to return to Kittyland where his skills and abilities were certainly needed. We miss him so much and we think about him every day, but we know that no friend or companion, no matter what type they are, stays in Humanland as long as any of us want them to. But we were fortunate to have known him for as long as we have. I don't know what our lives would have been like without Jekyll, but I know that we have been enriched by his presence. We can honestly say that Jekyll was quite unlike other kitties. The "stories" in this book are subjects that epitomized Jekyll's personality. He woke up happy, he loved to be clean, he made others smile, he showed up at our home office every day and was prepared to "work", he was a "Hero," he cared for those he loved, he was proud of who he was, and everything else that you have read about in this book. And yes, he honestly DID shake his booty! We learned so much from Jekyll, as have others. Now it is your turn. Please spend your life doing the things that "Jekyll Says ..."

In addition, if you can find it in your heart, please immediately travel to any kill shelter and adopt a homeless cat or dog and give him or her a loving home. You can do it.

Equally as important, please make the effort to adopt a vegan diet. It will be better for the environment, and it will be healthy for your body and mind. Understand this: Doing so will save the lives of thousands of innocent animals over the course of your lifetime.

The world will be a better place if you and others do the above. You can do it. Believe me.

D.C. Blackbird

About

About Jekyll

Jekyll began his career as a well-respected Supervisor in his Human's kitchen (when meals were being prepared). His attention to detail won him much praise from family and friends, and he was soon promoted to supervise his Humans in other endeavors throughout each and every room of their home. In the home office, he offered his unique perspective and invaluable advice to his Human Dad concerning important business decisions. Jekyll also contributed immensely to creative endeavors that his Human parents engaged in.

Currently, Jekyll is a well-respected professor of Catology and Humanology at Feline University in Kittyland, where he shares his extensive knowledge and valuable experience and all the important things that he learned while he visited Humanland.

About D.C. Blackbird

D.C. Blackbird is an American poet, songwriter, and author. D.C. is an advocate of animal adoption, care, liberation, rescue, rights, and welfare, as well as a proponent of Veganism. D.C. works closely with domestic and farm animals, and wildlife around the world, and is dedicated to telling stories about their experiences and adventures in Humanland, as well as their own Homelands.

About the Illustrator

Christine P. Flores is an Illustrator and Cartoonist. She loves and takes care of a special and beautiful blind cat named Bubux.

About the Graphic Designer

Leah Frieday is a creative designer with a full-sized furry and feather family. Her home is filled with great love from their weiner dog, Chanel, the 'Big Baby', Toupi and Binou, the kitty sisters, and Kiki the Cockatiel. All of her furry babies were found or were adopted. Rebecca, is Leah's daughter and she looks forward to a life of caring for, and protecting all precious beings in the animal kingdom.

Are you ready to learn even more from Jekyll and about Kittyland?
Please stay tuned, because more books and poems are coming
your way. You and your friends can order:

"Jekyll Says ..." and **"Jekyll Says More!"**
and **"Dreaming of Kittyland!"**

and other books from D.C. Blackbird from the same
place you ordered this book.

Jekyll Says ... visit **WelcomeToKittyland.com**

Campfire
Publishing

Made in the USA
Charleston, SC
30 December 2011